SCHIRMER'S LIBRARY
OF MUSICAL CLASSICS

Vol. 2118

THE FRENCH
PIANO COLLECTION

48 Pieces by

Chaminade

Couperin

Debussy

Fauré

Ravel

Satie

ISBN 978-1-4950-5161-6

G. SCHIRMER, *Inc.*

DISTRIBUTED BY

HAL•LEONARD®

7777 W. BLUEMOUND RD. P.O. BOX 13819 MILWAUKEE, WI 53213

www.musicsalesclassical.com
www.halleonard.com

CONTENTS

Sérénade

Edited and with fingering by
William Scharfenberg

Cécile Chaminade
Op. 29

Scarf-Dance

(Pas des Écharpes)

from *Cinq Airs de Ballet Callirhoë*

Edited and with fingering by
William Scharfenberg

Cécile Chaminade
Op. 37b, No. 2

Lolita
(Caprice Espagnol)

Edited and with fingering by
Louis Oesterle

Cécile Chaminade
Op. 54

Sœur Monique

from the eighteenth order of the *Third Book of Harpsichord Pieces*

François Couperin

★ May be omitted.

a) original

b) original

Suite in C minor

from the third order of the *First Book of Harpsichord Pieces*

François Couperin

"La Ténébreuse"

Courante

"La Lugubre"

Sarabande
Lento

Gavotte

Deux Arabesques
Première Arabesque

Claude Debussy

Tempo rubato *(un peu moins vite)* *(somewhat slower)*

Deuxième Arabesque

La plus que lente

Claude Debussy

42

Le petit nègre

Claude Debussy

a Tempo

ed espressivo

a Tempo

Children's Corner
I. Doctor Gradus ad Parnassum

Claude Debussy

Animato ma non troppo

Molto animato

II. Jimbo's Lullaby

III. Serenade for the Doll

IV. The snow is dancing

Poco rallentare

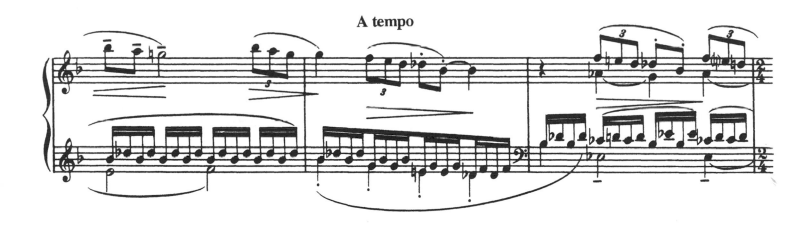

A tempo

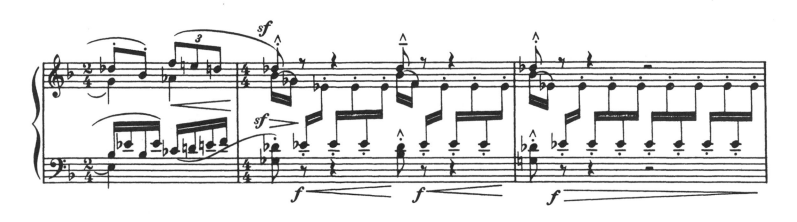

V. The little Shepherd

VI. Golliwogg's Cake-walk

Pour le piano
Prélude

Claude Debussy

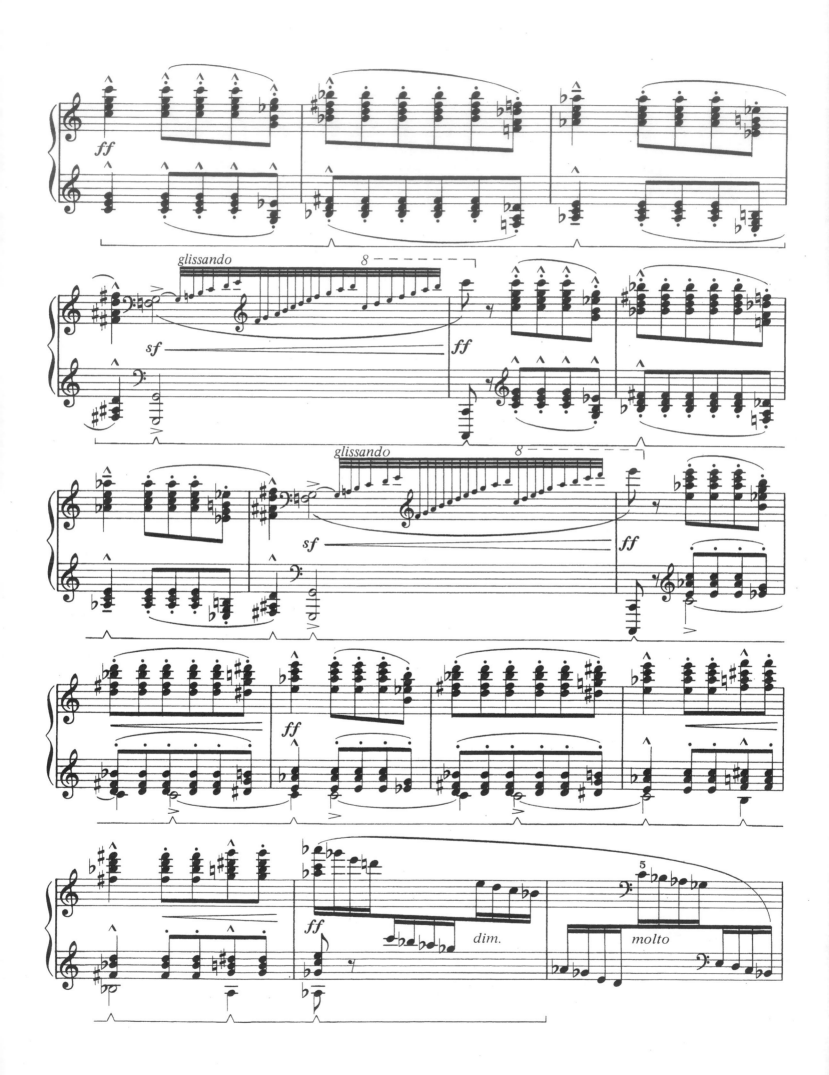

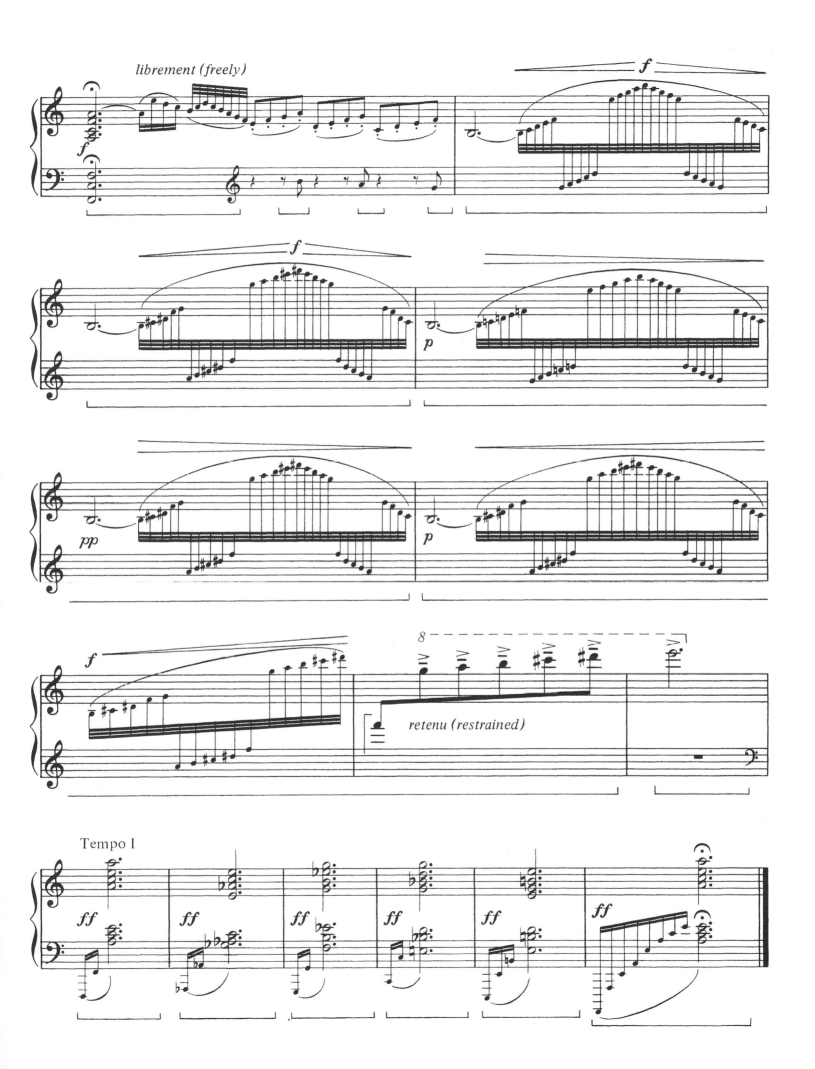

Sarabande

Avec une elegance grave et lente (elegantly, solemnly and slowly)

animez un peu (gradually faster)
très soutenu (very sustained)

au mouvt (first tempo)

u.c.

Toccata

peu a peu cre — scen — do

* arrangement pour petite mains (arrangement for small hands)

98

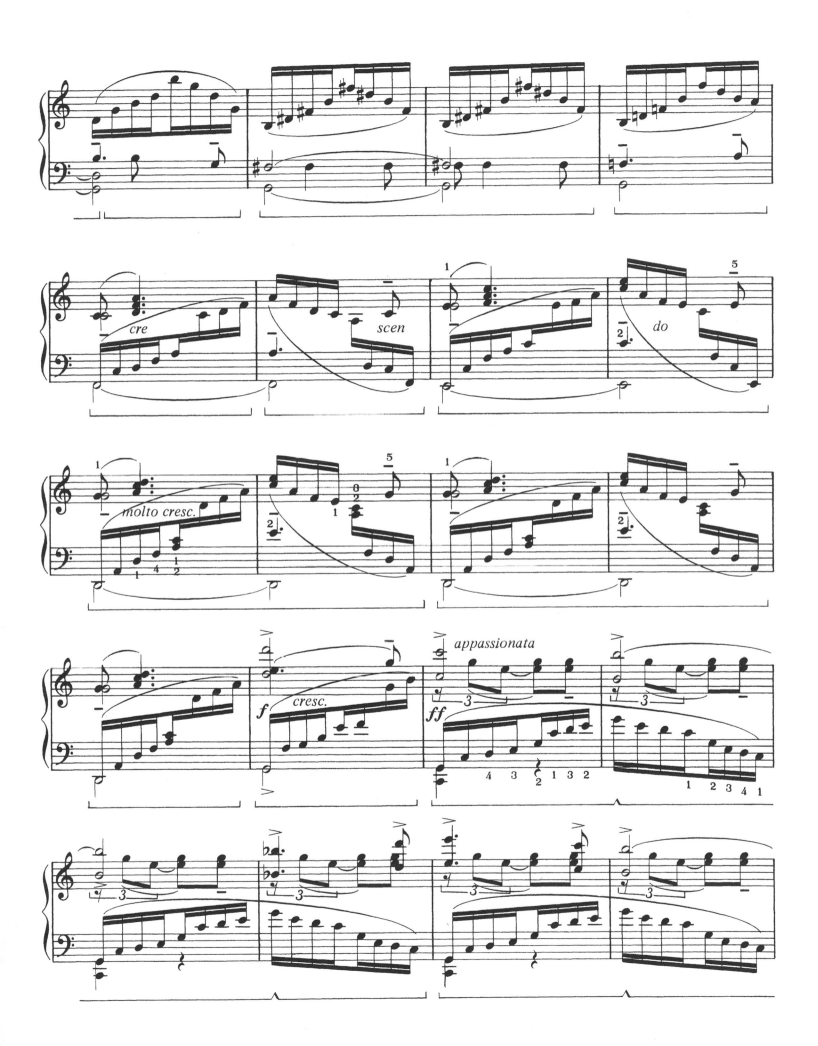

"Les sons et les parfums tournent dans l'air du soir"

from *Préludes*, Book I

Claude Debussy

a tempo

Plus lent

En animant

Cédez

Rubato

Serrez

Rubato

Serrez

la basse un peu appuyée et soutenue

Rubato

Serrez

m.d.

109

(..."Les sons et les parfums tournent dans l'air du soir")

Charles Baudelaire

Des pas sur la neige

from *Préludes*, Book I

Claude Debussy

(...Des pas sur la neige)

La fille aux cheveux de lin

from *Préludes*, Book I

Claude Debussy

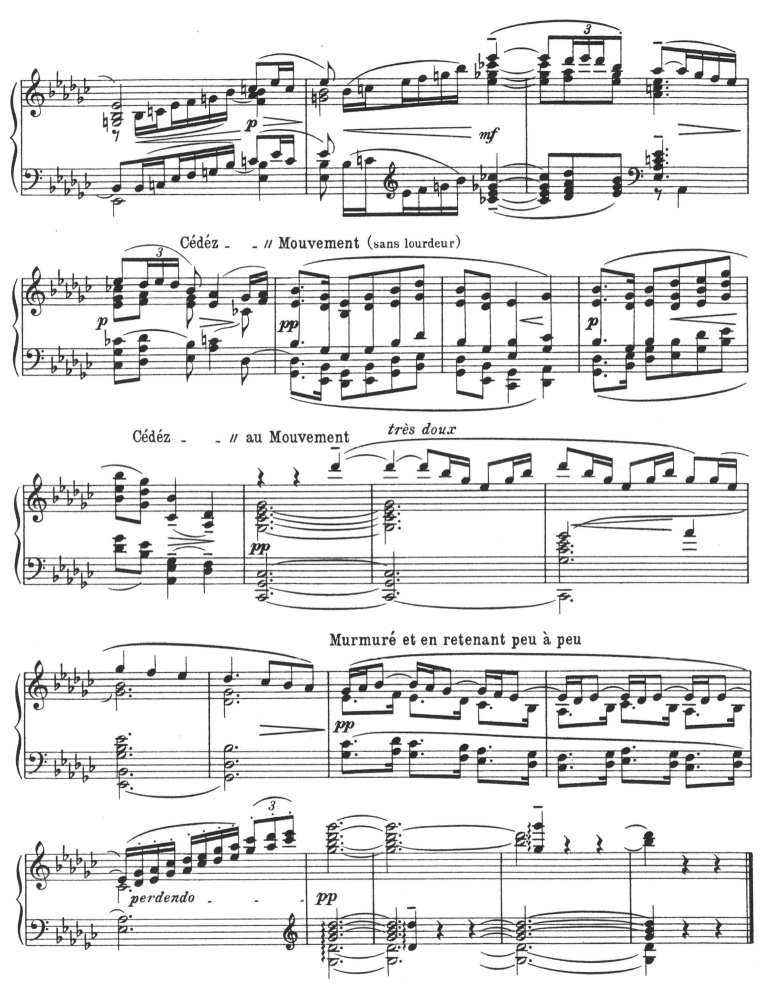

Cédéz _ _ // Mouvement (sans lourdeur)

Cédéz _ _ // au Mouvement *très doux*

Murmuré et en retenant peu à peu

(...La fille aux cheveux de lin)

Minstrels

from *Préludes*, Book II

Claude Debussy

(...Minstrels)

La Puerta del vino

from *Préludes*, Book II

Claude Debussy

Mouvement de Habanera
avec de brusques oppositions d'extrême
violence et de passionnée douceur

(...La Puerta del vino)

La terrasse des audiences du clair de lune

from *Préludes*, Book II

Claude Debussy

(...La terrasse des audiences du clair de lune)

La Cathédrale engloutie

from *Préludes*, Book I

Claude Debussy

Profondément calme (Dans une brume doucement sonore)

*) **Doux et fluide**

*)

*) Debussy, in his piano-roll recording (Welte-Mignon), played measures 7–12 and 22–83 in double speed.

Peu à peu sortant de la brume

Augmentez progressivement (Sans presser)

Sonore sans dureté

Un peu moins lent (Dans une expression allant grandissant)

au Mouvement

(...La Cathédrale engloutie)

Rêverie

Claude Debussy

132

Suite bergamasque
Prélude

Claude Debussy

Moderato *(tempo rubato)*

142

Menuet

Andante
pp *et très délicatement (very **soft** and delicately)*

Clair de lune

Passepied

cédez un peu
(*a little slower*)

a tempo

Impromptu in A-flat Major

Gabriel Fauré
Op. 34, No. 3

Nocturne in E-flat Major

Gabriel Fauré
Op. 36, No. 4

Berceuse in E Major

Gabriel Fauré
Op. 56, No. 1

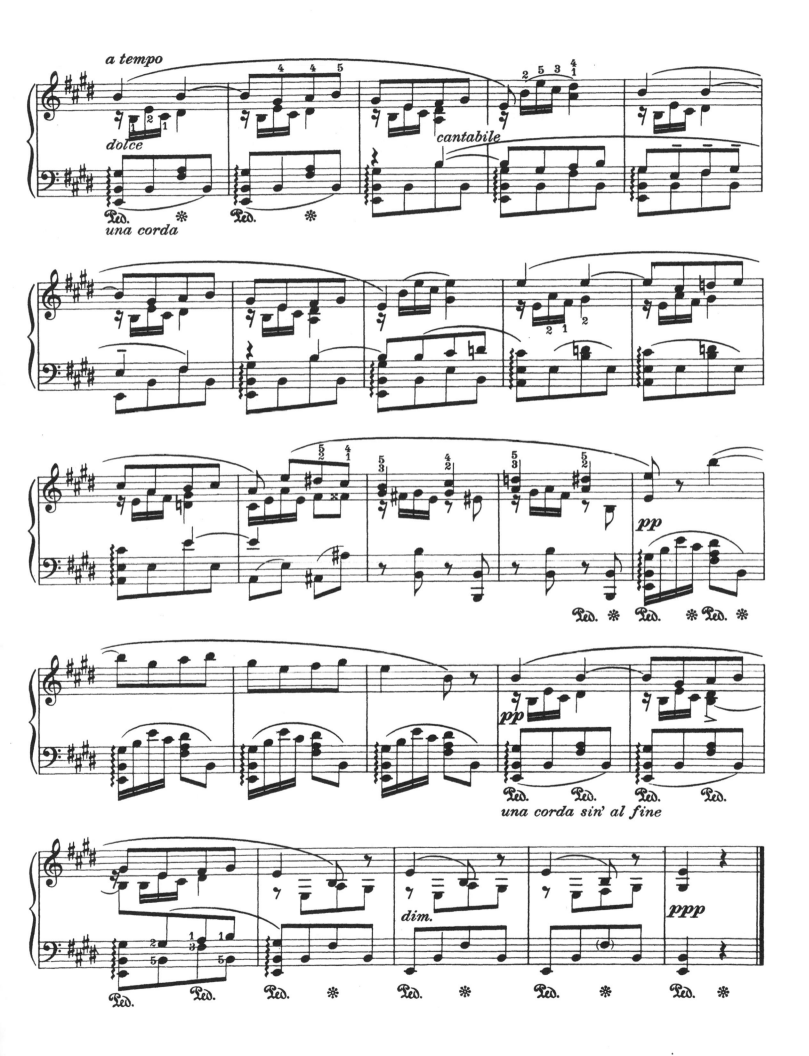

Improvisation in C-sharp minor

Gabriel Fauré
Op. 84, No. 5

Minuet on the Name of Haydn

Maurice Ravel

á Madame la Princesse E. de Polignac

Pavane for a Dead Princess
(Pavane pour une infante défunte)

Maurice Ravel

á Ida et Cipa Godebski

Sonatine

Maurice Ravel

I

II

Mouvement de Menuet (Minuet tempo)

un peu plus lent qu'au début
(a little slower than the beginning)

ra - len - tis - sez beaucoup
(retarding greatly)

très lent
(very slow)

rall.

III

Animé (Quickly)

très marqué (very accentuated)

Agité (Excitedly)

204

très marqué (very accentuated)

208

211

á Mademoiselle Jeanne de Bret

Three Gymnopédies*

Erik Satie

I

* Ceremonial choral dance performed at ancient Greek festivals.

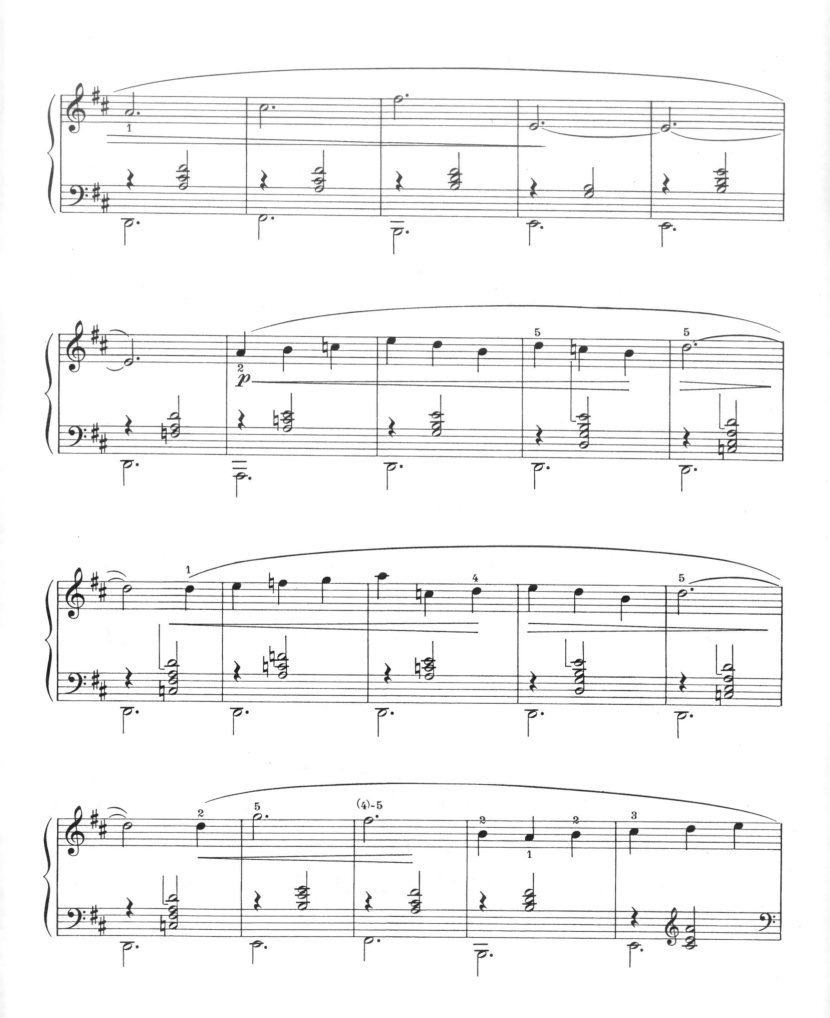

216

á Conrad Satie

II

á Charles Levade

III

for Roland Manuel

Gnossienne*

from *Three Gnossiennes*

Erik Satie

I

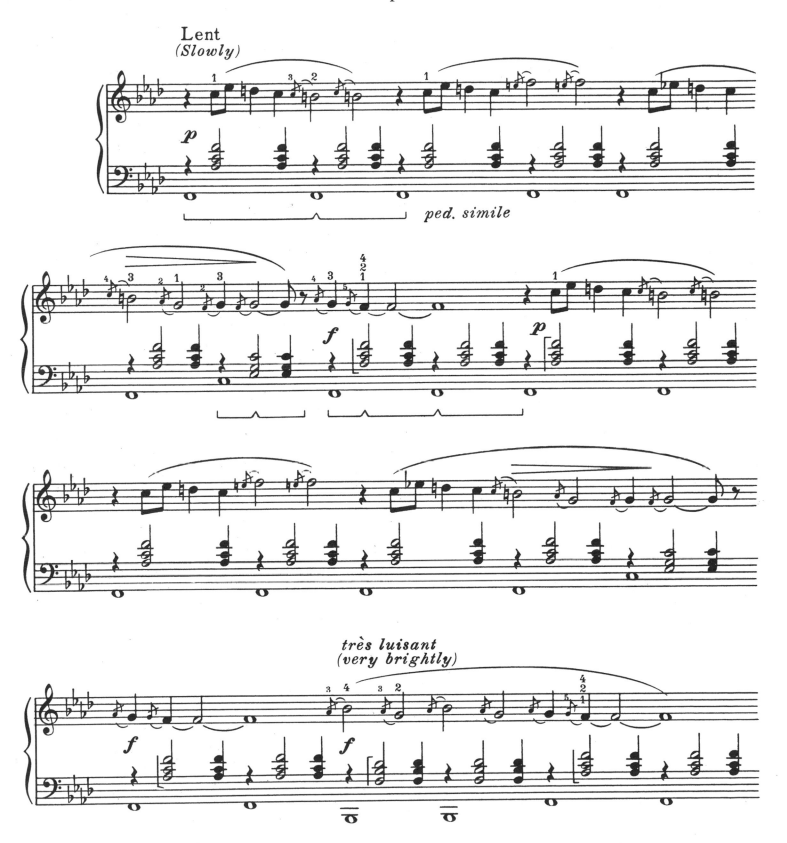

* The title is most likely a vague allusion to Cnossus, Knossos, or Gnossos, an ancient city on the island of Crete—the site of the palace of the mythical King Minos and the labyrinth where the Minotaur was confined— richly associated in ancient Greek mythology with Jupiter, Ariadne, and Theseus, the hero who slew the Minotaur.

postulez en vous-même
(make your own demands)

pas à pas
(little by little)

sur la langue
(on the tip of the tongue)

II

avec une légère intimité
(with a light intimacy)

sans orgueil
(without arrogance)

pp

III

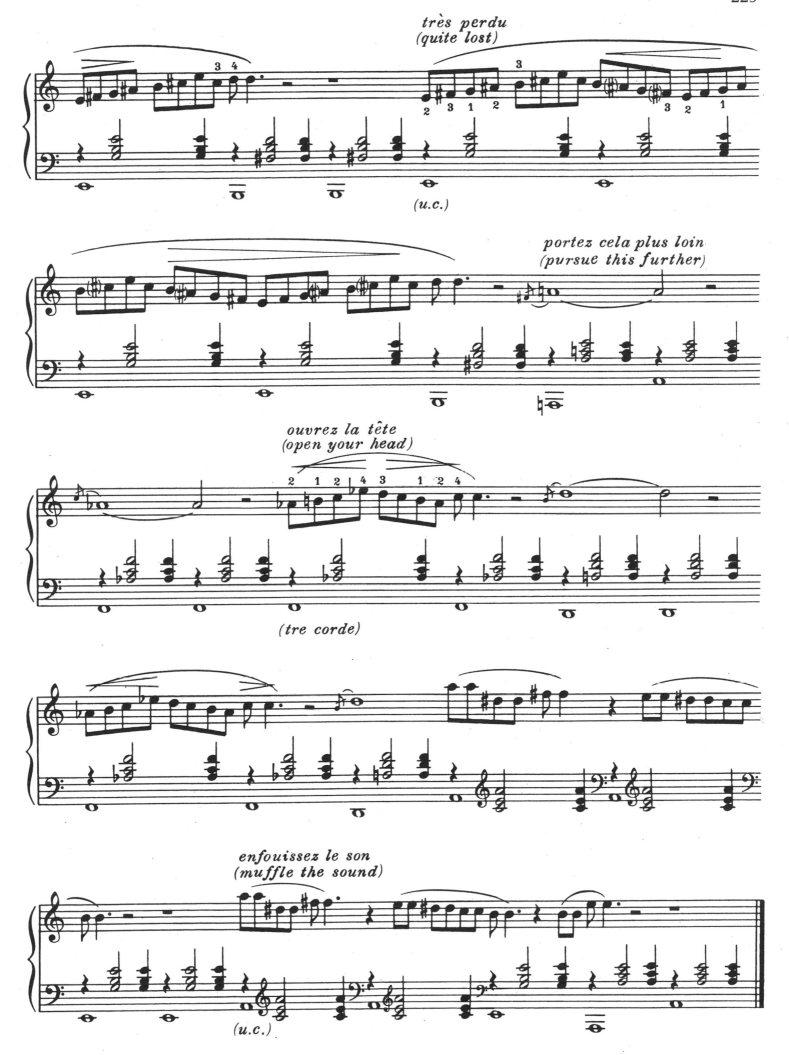